C000166112

HINDOO MYTHOLOGY

POPULARLY TREATED:

*BEING AN EPITOMIZED DESCRIPTION OF THE VARIOUS HEATHEN
DEITIES ILLUSTRATED ON THE SILVER SWAMI TEA SERVICE,*

PRESENTED AS A MEMENTO OF HIS VISIT TO INDIA

TO

H. R. H. THE PRINCE OF WALES, K.G., G.C.S.I.

BY

His Highness the Gaekwar of Baroda.

MADRAS :
PRINTED BY GANTZ BROTHERS,
ADELPHI PRESS, 7 & 8, MOUNT ROAD.
1875.

In the interest of creating a more extensive selection of rare historical book reprints, we have chosen to reproduce this title even though it may possibly have occasional imperfections such as missing and blurred pages, missing text, poor pictures, markings, dark backgrounds and other reproduction issues beyond our control. Because this work is culturally important, we have made it available as a part of our commitment to protecting, preserving and promoting the world's literature. Thank you for your understanding.

INDEX.

INDEX.

INTRODUCTION.

In the preparation of the following pages, it has been considered desirable to class the various subjects under the particular heads of which they form a part ;—namely, Siva the destroyer, Vishtnoo the preserver, and Brahma the creator. The difficulty in comprehending the various deities, contingent upon the many existing inconsistencies, not only of their respective titles, but also of the orthography of the names, has in a measure been met, by the insertion, under the same headings, of the different names appertaining to each *Swami*, together with the different modes of spelling the names. Should the perusal of these few pages excite a desire for further knowledge regarding the multifarious deities comprised in the Hindoo Pantheon, a study of " Moore's Hindoo Mythology," and the " Vishnu Puranas, translated by H. H. Wilson, Esq.," from whence many of the following particulars have been gathered, is calculated to afford much information relative to the subjects so briefly treated herein.

F. W. E.

SIVA *or* SIVEN.

Siva generally ranks as the highest deity although sometimes credited with a less exalted rank in the Hindoo Pantheon. He personifies destruction or reproduction, has neither beginning nor end, and is without outward form ; but is the distinguished possessor of four hands and arms, and has a centre eye placed in a perpendicular position in the forehead. He is usually represented riding on a bull, the emblem of divine justice, but occasionally appears in a standing posture, holding in one hand an antelope, and in the others are placed variously a trident, a boar's tusk, a rosary, a human skull, &c. A tiger's skin is wrapped around his loins, and the hide of an elephant furnishes him with a cloak. He is decorated with serpents, and garlands of skulls, bones, and the eyes of fishes. This deity is supposed to have once appeared as a mendicant in the Taruka forest. The wives of certain devotees resident there, fell in love with him and lost their virtue. Their lords greatly incensed, exerting their supernatural powers for the destruction of Siva, dug a pit from which issued a tiger which he slew and wrapped the skin round his loins; a deer followed, which he picked up and retained in his left hand; next a red hot iron bar, which he also seized and used as a weapon; then serpents, which he caught and hung about his person. He is likewise believed to have accomplished the destruction of an Asura who had obtained from Brahma a grant of victory over all gods, except Siva. He appeared in the form of an elephant, and forthwith proceeded to employ his strength, pursuing several Munis into a Siva temple, when the god rushed upon him; and after killing him, he stripped off his hide and threw it over his shoulders.

————:o:————

VEERABUTHREER, VEERABUTHREERSAWMY
or
VIRA BAHDRA.

Veerabuthreer.—Considerable variation exists in the accounts relative to the birth of this divinity. Some say that he sprung fully armed from Siva's central eye ; others that he was formed from a lock of hair plucked from that deity in rage ; whilst others assert that he was produced from a drop of Siva's sweat. Immediately succeeding his birth, he summoned legions of demons to his assistance and forthwith proceeded to destroy Dakshi's sacrifice. In the battle that ensued, Dakshi was decapitated, but on condition of his adoring Siva, he was permitted to substitute a goat's head in place of the lost member.

————:o:————

CAWLY *or* CAWLYUMMEN.

The Goddess Cawly, wife of Veerabuthreer, is also invoked as *Kali*, and *Durga;* names characteristic of some of the various forms she is in the habit of assuming. One of the most remarkable, though least pleasing, of her representations is that of Kali, which attitude she is believed to periodically adopt for the purpose of frightening sinners into repentance and virtue, and from its hideousness is well adapted to cause immediate terror. She is displayed with bending limbs and open hands with fingers lengthened and extended ; a serpent forms her girdle, and she appears in a state of nudity except a scanty cloth round her loins ; her belly is attenuated and shrivelled, her breasts pendent with long disgusting nipples, a serpent convolves round her neck, and turning on her bosom projects its head to support her protruding long rough tongue ; her chin is peaked, immense teeth and tusks are fixed in her lipless gums ; her nostrils and eyes are distended and bloated, and snakes form not altogether inappropriate ornaments for her ears, which are knotted in the pendent lobes, with heads raised and expanded hoods, and her hair is stiffened out to further illustrate her frightful glory. It is to this deity, in her character of Durga, that the annual festival of Ayuda or Durga Puja is held ; on which occasion the work of the clerk, the artizan and the laborer is suspended, and all combine to do honor to this deity by worshipping the books, the tools and instruments from which their subsistence is procured. Although human sacrifices have long since been prohibited, there is no doubt that to this goddess, in her character of Kali, they were formerly offered.

MAHADEVA.

Mahadeva is an assumed name of Siva, in which character he usually appears in the company of his consort Parvati, who is tendering him a cup of ambrosia. A chain of human skulls depends from his shoulders, whilst his neck, arms, and hair are encircled with serpents. A stream of water descending from his head on the Himalayas, and subsequently passing through a cow's mouth, is asserted to be the origin of the Ganges. This legend regarding the source of the sacred river, however, is disputed by the Vishnaivites, who aver that it proceeds from the nail of the great toe of Vishnu's left foot; whilst a third alleges that the Ganges threatened to overflow the earth, and at the intercession of the gods and sages, Siva compelled the great torrent to roll itself back again, and he enclosed the contracted waters in the crown tuft of his hair. Every tenth day this deity is anointed with an ointment compounded of oil, ghee, honey, cocoanut and cow's milk, carrots, rose-

water and various fruits, and afterwards borne with great
pomp and many signs of rejoicing through every street, city
and village.

——————:o:——————

GANESA, POLLEAR or GANAPATI.

——————

Ganesa, the first son of Mahadeva, is known as the god of
prudence and policy, or perhaps even more commonly
as the Belly-god.   His figure is of a particularly gross
and fanciful nature, having the head of an elephant attached
to an exceedingly corpulent exterior.   Although Mahadeva
is his reputed father, the legend regarding his existence
states, that he was formed of fair proportions by his mother
Parvati, from certain excrementitious particles and impu-
rities of her own body, at which Mahadeva was jealous and
displeased.   Ganesa was his mother's champion, vindicating
her honor and rights on all occasions, even against the
infringement of Vishnu and his mother's lord.   On one
occasion Vishnu and Ganesa fought, and the latter would

have conquered, but for the interposition of Siva, who cut
off Ganesa's head. At this his mother was greatly distressed,
and threatened to derange the destinies of the universe if her son was not restored to her. To prevent
this threat being carried out, and at the supplication of the
congregated deities, Siva consented to his restoration, but
on searching for the decapitated head, it could nowhere be
found, and it was accordingly resolved to fix up on the head-
less trunk, the head of the first animal that made its appearance. This happened to be an elephant, and the resolu-
tion having been carried into effect, resulted in the adoption
of Ganesa by Siva. Ganesa is invoked prior to the com-
mencement of any and every undertaking, and in September of each year the festival of Polleyar Chalhurtti is
observed, as a general holiday, by every class of the native
community. Temporary images of the deity, formed of clay
or cowdung, are then paraded through the streets, followed
by vast crowds of his admirers, and he is propitiated by
immense quantities of sweetmeats and cakes.

VENAYAGUR.

Venayagur is an assumed name of the preceding deity, whose mission was the destruction of Gayanu Gasura; an elephant-faced giant who had obtained by severe penance, a promise from Siva that the gods should be subservient to his will, that he should be incapable of being wounded by any weapon, and that he should not be destroyed either by gods, men, or animals. In consequence of his cruelty, the gods betook themselves to Siva for protection, and this deity, together with his wife, whilst on the slopes of the Himalayas, assumed the form of a male and female elephant, from which was instantly born the elephant-faced deity, being neither god, man, or beast—yet all combined. Assuming the command of the celestial bands, he departed to combat the monster. Bearing in mind his father's promise, he used no ordinary weapon, but broke off his right tusk and cast it at his adversary. The giant immediately changed his form into a rat, when Venayagur leaped upon him and used him as a vehicle, in which position he is most commonly depicted. He is as yet unmarried, but is still in search of a bride, and for that purpose sits at the corners of streets and at the threshholds of temples on the alert. His vehicle is variously spoken of as a bandycoot (rat), rabbit or mouse, and in his numerous representations, it perhaps bears an equal resemblance to either.

——————:o:——————

SOOBRAMANIAH, SOOBRAMANIAN
or
SOOBRAMANIYA.

———————

Soobramaniah is known only by the above appellatives in Southern India, and in some portions of the Bombay Presidency. In other parts he is known as Kartikeya. He is believed to have had no mother, but to have proceeded from his father Mahadeva alone : and was discovered on the banks of the Ganges by the six daughters of as many Rajahs, who, each claimed him as her son, and the whole offered him their breasts. The child at once assumed six mouths and received nourishment from each. He is credited with the destruction of Tripurasura after a conflict of ten days, and the consequent restoration of tranquillity and order throughout the world. He has numerous adherents, and amongst others he is worshipped by the Comatte or Chetty caste, who annually proceed to various places where snakes are known to abound, and there deposit milk and eggs to feed them, with the view of propitiating the god. Star feast, the popular festival of the general followers of this deity, occurs every twenty-seventh day which is observed as a fast day till the evening when they commence taking food. Others of his disciples observe a similar fast six days subsequent to each new and full moon, and on the evening of the last day a grand exhibition of fireworks is displayed bringing the feast to a close.

———:o:———

PULANIONDY.

Pulaniondy, an adopted name of Soobramaniah, derived from Pullany, the mountain on which he is supposed to reside.

EASVEREN.

Easveren, a further representation of Siva, in which he is depicted riding on a nandi or white bull, which is understood to be the personification of divine justice.

————:o:————

EASVERY.

Easvery, the reputed wife of Easveren, who is supposed to be riding on a tiger, her favorite mode of locomotion.

————:o:————

AROOMOOGASWAMY, or ARUMUGAN.

Aroomoogaswamy is the second son of Siva, whose distinguishing attributes are six faces and twelve arms. He assumed command of the heavenly armies, and accompanied by hosts of goblins and imps, proceeded to make war on the Asuras. He appropriated to himself many forms, including those of a lion and tiger, and subsequently that of a mango tree, and discharging his lance divided the tree in two parts, one part taking the form of a cock and the other a peacock. He is supposed to be riding on the latter.

------:o:------

THAIVANNY.

Thaivanny, the second wife of Soobramaniah, is stated to be the daughter of the white elephant of Indra.

------:o:------

MAURIUMMEN.

Mauriummen is depicted riding on a two-winged lion. She is the supposed daughter of a devotee and his wife. The legend asserts that the latter, by her chastity, transformed Siva, Vishtnoo and Brahma into children. On their subsequent restoration to their primitive state, they cursed the woman declaring that her daughter should be born in the house of a washerman, and be worshipped exclusively by low caste people. In Southern India Mauriummen is invoked as the goddess of small-pox, which she inflicts and likewise removes.

VULLIUMMEN.

Vulliummen, the wife of Soobramaniah, is a descendant of the Koraver or hunting caste, and is represented riding on the back of an elephant.

———:o:———

SABAPATHY.

Sabapathy is another representation of Siva, who appears dancing and otherwise catering for the amusement of his followers; manifestly in the destruction of Sooren, whom he is trampling beneath his feet.

———:o;———

GOORUMOORTHUM.

Goorumoorthum.—Guru signifies spiritual teacher, and in this character Goorumoorthum appears for the purpose of imparting theological instruction to the four sons of Brahma who were pantheists.

THUTCHANMOORTHY.

Thutchanmoorthy also appears as a tutor to instruct the sons of Brahma in the end portions of the Vedas.

————:o:————

THAVANTHIREN, *or* INDRA.

Thavanthiren, the recognised king of deities, is the distinguished possessor of a thousand eyes, and his supposed residence is in heaven. He is divided in his belief, and worships. both Vishtnoo and Siva. His favorite mode of locomotion is a white elephant. The great Pungul feast is annually held in his honor, when he is supplicated and invoked by offerings of the choicest first fruits of the year.

————:o:————

MAGADASOORA SUMMARUM.

Magadasoora Summarum represents a giant who appropriated the form of a bull, and fought with, but was defeated and slain by the wife of Siva.

SUNGARUM.

Sungarum denotes beauty, and the figure bearing this name is not a swamy, but is depicted riding on an imaginary beast, having the head of a woman, wings of a bird, and the body of a cow with two tails.

————:o:————

MUTHOORAVEEREN.

Muthooraveeren was the son of the king of Benares. At his birth, the astrologers admonished his father to remove the child from the town to prevent its being burnt. Instructions to this effect were accordingly issued, and as the child was lying asleep in a jungle, whither he had been transported, he was discovered by the wife of a cobbler by whom he was nursed and brought up. On his arriving at manhood, he seduced away the daughter of a king called Bommanan. With her he departed south as far as Madura, where he was placed by the king of Madura at the head of his troops for the destruction of the notorious robbers of that district.   He accomplished this commission, and subsequently stole away a second damsel named Velliummen, and having been captured and punished, he terminated his existence by cutting his throat.   His principal temple is at Madura, built to perpetuate his deeds of valour.

————:o:————

THEROOCKOORIPPOOTHONDUR.

————

Theroockoorippoothondur, a washerman who merited heaven by gratuitously washing the clothes of the devotees of Siva.

————:o:————

BHAIRAVA.

————

Bhairava, another son of Siva, produced from the breath of that deity, is worshipped principally by the Mahrattas.   He is occasionally considered as an Avatara of Siva.   His name is derived from Bheru, meaning the terrific, and in pictures he is represented holding a ghastly head, and a cup of blood, attended by two dogs apparently in anticipation of sharing the horrid repast.

CARICALAMMAY.

Caricalammay, a female devotee and disciple of Siva, who, for the sake of her religion, abandoned her husband together with her immense wealth, and thereby obtained the distinguished title of the "Mother of Siva."

————:o:————

SOOREN *and* PUCKAHSOOREN.

The figures thus designated are not representations of deities, but the appellatives are somewhat general vernacular terms, denoting the numerous adversaries of the respective Swamies and their disciples.

VISHTNOO, or MAHAVISHTNOO.

Vishtnoo, the second person of the Hindoo triad, has no fewer than a thousand names, and claims to be the personification of the Sun, or rather, according to the Hindoo belief, the Sun is the personification of Vishtnoo. He is credited with the ability to transform himself into the various elements of earth, air, and water, and it is narrated that, when the whole earth was under water and Vishnoo lay asleep on the Devi (island), a lotus grew from his navel, the flower of which reached the surface of the flood; that Brahma originated from the flower, and viewing the broad expanse, believed himself to be the first-born, and accordingly entitled to usurp precedence above all future beings. He, however, resolved to investigate the deep to ascertain if any being existed in it who had a prior claim to pre-eminence, and accordingly descended by the stalk of the lotus, and finding Vishtnoo asleep, loudly demanded who he was. Vishtnoo replied that *he* was the first-born, which being denied by Brahma, a battle ensued, when Mahadeva appearing on the scene, asserted *his* claim to be the first-born, but willing to relinquish his pretensions to whichever of the contending parties, succeeded in viewing the summit of his (Mahadeva's) head or the soles of his feet. Brahma instantly ascended to the regions of immensity, till being fatigued, he descended; claiming to have discovered the top of Mahadeva's head and called as his witness, the first-born cow. This assumption, Mahadeva declared a falsehood, stating that the mouth of the cow should be defiled and that Brahma should perform no sacred rites. Vishtnoo who had gone in an opposite direction, also returned, acknowledging that he had failed to obtain a sight of the soles of Mahadeva's feet; who thereupon affirmed him the first-born among gods and supreme over all. Vishnu is the alleged possessor of four hands, and is generally depicted supporting a chank (a kind of shell,) in one hand, in another a wheel, from which irresistible flames of fire is supposed to issue, whilst his remaining arms are brought forward over the breast. His color is green, and he bears the enviable reputation of being the most beautiful amongst gods or men. He has ten incarnations, which include five human forms, to-gether with those of a fish, a tortoise, a pig, a lion and a horse, to the latter however he has not yet attained. A variety of feasts in honour of Vishtnoo are yearly celebrated. The principal to commemorate the birth of Krishna takes place about the end of August, when offerings of butter and milk are freely made. Another is celebrated in December, known as the Yagathasy festival, when his followers abstain both from food and sleep for a space of twenty-four hours.

————:o:————

MUTCHAVATHARUM *or* MATSYA.

————

Mutchavatharum, the first incarnation of Vishtnoo in com-mon with the other attributes of the same deity, is re-presented with four arms. He has the body and tail of a fish ; which form he is believed to have assumed on the oc-casion of the universe being submerged with water. Manu, the seven Rishis, and their respective wives alone escaped the general destruction, and they were ordered to enter a large ship together with pairs of all kinds of animals. Vishtnoo having adopted the form above described, commanded the ship to be fastened by a cable formed of a huge serpent to his stupendous horn and secured thereto till the flood subsided. Being desirous of offspring, he diligently performed a sacrifice, and after a year, a female was produced who came to him, and in reply to his enquiry " who art thou," answered that she was his daughter. He further enquired how such could be the case, and was assured that she was begotten from the clarified butter, thick milk, whey and curds that he had so devoutly offered in the water. She asserted her ability to confer blessings, and by her he possessed the coveted offspring, and what further blessings he desired were all granted to him.

———:o:———

COORMA AVATHARUM.

Coorma Avatharum, the second grand avatara of Vishtnoo, is illustrated in the form of a tortoise, and his history, together with the preceding, seems to point somewhat imperfectly and indefinitely to the Deluge. The disciples of

Siva assert that with the view of restoring to mankind some of the comforts lost to them in the flood, Vishtnoo became incarnate in the shape of a tortoise, that he supported the mountain Mandara on his back to create an axis whereon the gods and demons, the serpent Vasuki serving as a rope, churned the ocean for the recovery of the lost beverage of immortality. The adherents of Vishtnoo, on the contrary, allege that the Asuras and deities placed a large mountain into the milky sea and bound it with a cobra. The Asuras pulled the reptile by the tail, and the gods by the head, for the purpose of extracting butter from the sea, but the mountain being too ponderous for the cobra, Vishtnoo, in the form of a tortoise, supported the mountain from underneath. The legend, however, fails to further enlighten the uninitiated into the supposed benefits arising from the deity's transformation.

————:o:————

VARAGA AVATHARUM.

Varaga Avatharum, is the third illustrious attribute of Vishtnoo, whose prominent feature is a boar's head, supported on human shoulders. It is reported that

Brahma promised a religious fanatic named Hiranayaksha to grant him any request he might make, who thereupon desired to be exempt from certain noxious animals which he enumerated, omitting the hog. After securing his request, Hiranayaksha became excessively wicked and presumptuous, to such an extent as to seize the earth and to carry it with him into the sea. Vishtnoo at once assumed the form of the boar, a symbol of strength, dived into the waters, and after a fearful contest of a thousand years, conquered the wicked one and restored the earth on the point of his tusks. Another version of this remarkable transformation is, to the effect that Vishtnoo emanated from Brahma's nostrils in the form of a pig, and naturally grew to a boar.

------:o:------

NARASIMMA.

Narasimma, the fourth avatara of Vishtnoo, is a monstrous and somewhat remarkable combination of a lion with a human form. He is commonly delineated sitting in a cleft pillar in the act of tearing in pieces Hiranayakasipa, a wicked king, who, after having obtained from Brahma universal monarchy, exemption from death, either by God or man, or by any animal, by day or night, within doors or without, in heaven or in earth ; adopted a spirit of arrogance and presumption, and his impiety being insufferable Vishtnoo incarnated as a lion, after an hour's conflict conquered and destroyed him. The chief temple of this deity is at Chingleput, near Madras.

————:o:————

VAMUNA *or* VAMINA AVATHARUM.

Vamuna, the fifth incarnation of Vishtnoo, appears as a dwarf, shading himself with an umbrella, whilst king Maha Bali is pouring water over his extended hand ; thereby ratifying his oath to grant him the sovereignty of the universe, including the three regions of earth, heaven, and hell. The legend avers that Vishtnoo appropriated this exterior with the object of punishing the king for neglecting the essential ceremonies and offerings to the deities. In this form he represents Kasyapa, the younger brother of Indra, and presenting himself before Maha Bali, desired as much space as he could span in three strides. The king somewhat chagrined at the modest request of the diminutive stranger, urged him to make a further petition for something more worthy of him to bestow. From this arose the application for universal sovereignty, and as the water fell on his hands, the dwarf expanded till he filled the world, and Vishtnoo thus manifesting himself, deprived Bali at two steps of heaven and earth; but the king, on the whole, being a virtuous monarch, was allowed to retain Patala, or hell, still in his dominions.

————:o:————

PARASU RAMA, BALARAMA AVATHRUM.

Parasu Rama, the sixth power attributed to Vishtnoo, is holding in his hand a somewhat rude description of axe. He is the reputed son of Jamadagni and his wife Renuka, and is believed to have been born near Agra. His chroniclers state that Renuka, in the absence of her sons, who had gone to gather fruit, went forth to bathe.

On her way to the stream she beheld the Prince of Muttikavati, with a garland of lotuses on his neck, sporting with his Queen in the water, and felt envious of their felicity. Defiled by unworthy thoughts, she returned disquieted to the hermitage, and her husband perceived her agitation. Beholding his wife fallen from perfection and shorn of the lustre of her sanctity, Jamadagni reproved her, and was exceeding wrath. His four sons returning from the woods, on entering, were successively commanded by the father to put their mother to death. Amazed and influenced by natural affection, they made no reply, upon which Jamadagni becoming angry, cursed them, and they became idiots. Lastly, Parasu Rama returning, his father likewise commanded him to kill his mother, who had sinned, and to execute the foul deed without repining. Rama accordingly lifted the axe and beheaded his mother, upon which Jamadagni's wrath was assuaged, and being gratified with his son's obedience, said, since thou hast obeyed my commands and hast performed that which was difficult to be fulfilled, demand from me whatever blessings thou wilt, and thy desires shall be gratified. Rama at once solicited the restoration of his mother to life, with forgetfulness of her having been slain, purification from all defilement, the return of his brothers to reason, and for himself invincibility in single combat and length of days. All these things did his father bestow, and after a life spent in mighty and holy deeds, Rama gave his entire property in alms, and retired to a district between Surat and the Southern Cape where he is said to still exist.

————:o:————

RAMER or RAMA.

Rama, the seventh special manifestation of Vishtnoo, derived his popularity from being a successful warrior and conqueror. His chroniclers allege that he killed a giantess, and a savage, by means of supernatural arms. Sita became his consort, but Ravana, a demon king of Ceylon, becoming enamoured of her, carried her off through the air. Rama eventually discovered her place of captivity, and with the assistance of Hanuman and Sugriva, accomplished the destruction of Ravana and recovered Sita, who was afterwards subjected to the ordeal of fire, to convince the world of her chaste escape from the hands of her captor. Subsequently in a fit of jealousy of a fanciful nature, he sent her away from him into a wilderness, where she was delivered of twin sons. A horse belonging to Ramer, who in the meantime had claimed to be emperor of the world, was seized by his sons, and when attempting to recover the horse, the sons were recognized by their father, which resulted in a reconciliation between the parents.

———:o:———

KRISHNA.

Krishna, the eighth incarnation of Vishtnoo, an exceedingly popular deity, is represented in a variety of gymnastic attitudes and grotesque characters. He also commonly appears as a musician, playing on the flute and standing upon a serpent. His parents were Vasudeva and Deavki. When an infant he escaped the general destruction of all infants; commanded by Kansas, and was brought up by an honest herdsman and his wife; and passed his juvenile days, dancing, sporting and piping in the company of a multitude of young milkmaids, from whom he selected nine as favorites. He is stated to have slain Naraka, a five-headed Asura, and to have taken possession of his wealth, including elephants, horses and women. The latter numbered 16,000, the whole of whom Krishna subsequently married, multiplying himself into as many distinct forms, that each maiden believed he had married her in his single person. He abode severally in the dwelling of each of his wives, who each bore him ten sons, and believed herself to be the exclusive favourite of her lord. To corroborate the existence of Krishna in this multiplicity of forms, it is related that Narada, his musical associate, having no wife, or substitute, intimated to his friend the feasibility of sparing him one from his long catalogue of ladies. Krishna generously told him to win and wear any one he chose not immediately in requisition for himself. Narada accordingly departed wooing from house to house till he had exhausted the whole, in each of which Krishna was discovered. A famous representation of this deity is in the character of a guardian to certain herdsmen; to deliver them from the vengeance of Indra, who being jealous of the adoration paid to Krishna, threatened a partial deluge, whereupon the latter lifted the mountain Govarddhana and supported it on the point of his little finger above his head, and invited the shepherds to take shelter underneath. The morals of Krishna appear to have been of a somewhat questionable character. In his numerous representations he is seldom seen unattended by a female, sometimes sitting in a kind of swing with Radha, his favorite mistress; and in others encircled with a number of supposed virgins which the legend asserts had assembled to celebrate in mirth and sport the advent of Krishna, who himself appearing in their midst, proposed a dance, and to meet the deficiency of partners divided himself into as many portions as there were damsels.

BUDDHA *or* POWTHA AVATHARUM.

Buddha is the ninth attribute of Vishtnoo. The worship of this deity has become almost obsolete in India ; but in Burmah and China he has still numerous disciples and adherents. His mother's name was Maya, and his birth was inaugurated by the presence of 40,000 deities, who received him on a golden net, from which he was transferred to a tiger's skin, and subsequently consigned to the care of the nobles. Buddha being independent of them, leapt upon the ground, and wherever his feet touched a lotus grew. His life appears to have been one of more than ordinary hardship and privation; his home being a desert of undulating plains, and his food the unsavory mixture of a beggar's store. Having first conquered quality in his daily fare, he afterwards brought himself to exist on a pepper corn a day. He is generally illustrated as a naked mendicant, which form he assumed for the protection of the deities, who had been worsted in a conflict with some giants or demons. He died of diarrhœa, the effects of eating pork served to him by a worthy smith; Buddha having previously relinquished his peppercorn nourishment for food of a more substantial nature. At his death his successor approached to do obeisance to his sacred feet, and was followed in this act of reverence by five hundred other priests. The feet of the corpse protruded from their bandages to meet their reverential gestures, which being concluded, they quietly withdrew, and the pyre spontaneously burst into flames, although it had twice previously resisted attempts to ignite it.

---:o:---

KALKI or CALLICKA.

Kalki, the tenth and last manifestation of Vishtnoo, has yet to be attained. This event is prophesied to take place at the end of the present or Kali age; Vishtnoo will then appear riding a white-winged horse with a drawn scimitar in his hand, and will renovate the creation and inaugurate an era of purity.

VENKATACHELLAPATHY.

Veucatachella signifies mountain, and the above is an adopted name of Vishtnoo during his residence there.

———:o:———

WOODYAVUR.

Woodyavur, the first disciple of Vishtnoo, is depicted in a cross-legged position, seated on the skin of a tiger with his hands in an attitude of devotion.

———:o:———

ANOOMAUR or HANUMAN.

Hanuman, or the " Monkey god," is likewise a disciple of Vishtnoo. He is believed to have mistaken the sun for a sweatmeat and to have swallowed it. His mother is reported to have formed an illicit connection with Prabanjana, and was excluded from her house and home for her bad behaviour. Subsequent to her transgression Anoomaur was born to her ; but was acknowledged and brought up by his father. Hanuman's visit to Ceylon in search of Sita, the wife of Ramer, is perhaps the most interesting portion of his somewhat extended history. A difficulty arose as to the best means of crossing the straits to Ceylon, when various monkeys volunteered to jump across, but Anoomaur was the only one capable of accomplishing the feat. Having discovered Sita, he offered to transport her at once on his back to the presence of her husband, to which she modestly replied that she could not voluntarily touch the person of any but her husband. He then re-assured her and afterwards defeated an army of 80,000 men sent against him by Ravana, the captor of Sita. He was also successful in four other encounters, but was eventually captured and commanded to be put to death. The sentence was subsequently revoked, and Ravana ordered his tail to be set on fire, when Anoomaur escaping from his guards, succeeded in setting the city on fire, and accomplished the complete destruction of Ravana, and restored Sita to her husband.

GEROODEN *or* GARUDA.

Garuda is an animal, half bird, half man, and is the vehicle of Vishtnoo, who is generally seated on and bestriding his shoulders with his legs in front and Garuda holding the rider by the ankles.

———:o:———

GOTHUNDAPAUNEE.

Gothundapaunee is an adopted name of Vishtnoo, derived from Gothundum, the name of the bow he is supposed to be carrying in his hand.

———:o:———

VENNY KRISTNAN.

Venny Kristnan, a juvenile appellation of Krishna. Venny is derived from butter, of which Krishna in his youthful days was decidedly partial. He is represented bearing a ladder, which he is supposed to have utilised to reach the jar from which he stole his neighbour's butter. He was discovered inside the jar and a plate was placed at the mouth to prevent his escape, whilst the owner hastened to report the fact to his parents, but on arrival, found the juvenile offender had arrived first and was playing with his mother. He is also accused of having pilfered and ate his play-fellows curds, and being reproved by his foster mother, he desired her to examine his mouth, in which, to her amazement, she beheld the whole universe in all its completeness of magnificence.

————:o:————

CARLINGA MIRTHUNUM.

Carlingum and Balakristnan are further juvenile titles, and represent a few of the many characters assumed by Krishna, to which the preceding history will apply.

————:o:————

YESOTHY or YASADO.

Yasado, wife of a herdsman and foster mother of Krishna.

ARJOONAUM *or* ARJUNA.

Arjuun, is credited with the performance of the obsequial rites at the death of Krishna. He is divided in his belief and worships both Vishtnoo and Siva.

———:o:———

RUNGANATHUR *or* RAMANUJA.

Ramanuja was born at Sri Permatoor, near Madras, and immortalised his existence by his zeal and diligence in inculcating the Vishnuvite faith. He established as many as 700 colleges, mostly situated in Southern India, and many of the temples which had been perverted to the worship of Siva, he restored to their primitive character. He defied the command of the Chola king, who was a bigoted worshipper of Siva, to subscribe to that declaration of faith, and in consequence was compelled to abandon his home at Sri Rangum, and lived till the death of the king in the Mysore country, after which he returned to his home, and his principal temple there still exists.

GAJENTHRAMOORTCHUM.

Gajenthramoortchum, a disciple of Vishtnoo, on being cursed by a certain devotee, was transformed into an elephant. When drinking water at a well, a crocodile, also a former disciple of Vishtnoo, and indebted to the Rishi for his metamorphosed condition, caught hold of the elephant and pulled him into the well. After a struggle of a thousand years, the elephant becoming very weak, called upon the gods for assistance, and was answered by none but Vishtnoo, who rescued the elephant and cut the throat of the crocodile.

———:o:———

PARTHASARTHY.

Parthasarthy, a transformation of Krishna, is represented with a whip in his hand. He distinguished himself in the great war of the Mahabharata where he was employed as coachman by Parthen, the third son of Pandoo. His chief temple is at Triplicane, Madras. His disciples honor him by fasting on four succeeding Saturdays during a part of the months of September and October of each year, on which occasions his worship is conducted in all Vishnuvite temples.

————:o:————

MUNMATHUN *or* MUNMATHA.

Munmatha, the God of Love, is the reputed son of Vishtnoo. He is represented riding through the air, kneeling on the back of a bird, and is in the act of directing his arrow at Siva, for which act of presumption he is reduced to ashes by fire that proceeded from the eye of the enraged deity. He was however subsequently restored to existence on the intercession of Parvati, the bride of Mahadeva. His principal worshippers are the Guzerattis and Rajpoots. They manufacture, and worship an image of Munmatha, from the new to the full moon, on the last day of which they burn it, in the meantime colored waters are freely sprinkled by both sexes over their friends and relatives. He is likewise invoked by damsels desirous of securing faithful partners.

VARUTHARAJASAWMY.

Varuther, Vicoonthavasee, Moogunden and Vanoogopaul, are assumed names and minor Avataras of Vishtnoo, each representing a separate character and delineation of this capricious deity.

———:o:———

PEROOMAL.

This title also includes Veeraragavaperoomal, Vencatasaperoomal and Thoolasingaperoomal, all of which illustrate the varied, though less important transformation of Vishtnoo, of whose history they form a part.

———:o:———

WOOPAMANIAR.

Woopamaniar, a sage and also high priest, is illustrated in the act of baptising Krishna, the ninth incarnation of Vishtnoo.

BRAMAH or BRAHMA.

R**rahma's** position as one of the three heads comprising
the Hindoo Trinity, is popularly believed to be in-
ferior to that of either Siva or Vishtnoo. This, perhaps, is due to the fact that no temples are dedicated
exclusively to his service, and he has consequently a fewer
number of disciples. His images, however, find a place in
the temples of other deities, and he is there worshipped by
his adherents and reverentially propitiated by offerings and
supplications. He is the recognized "God of creation,"
and although his creative power is now dormant, his disciples
aver that at some future time it will again be called into
action. Brahma is the supposed author of a compilation of
prayers called the four Vedas. He is most commonly represented with four heads, and a Veda is alleged to have
emanated from each mouth. Another legend asserts that
he formerly possessed five heads, one of which he lost in a
hostile encounter with Siva, whilst another states, that in
the North-west of India, in the vicinity of Cashmir, he

assumed a mortal shape, and one-half of his body issued from him without any diminution having been experienced ; he forthwith framed of it a damsel named Satarapa. She being excessively comely, he fell in love with her, but having originated from his body, he considered her his daughter, and was ashamed. During the conflict between guilt and love, he remained motionless, with his eye fixed upon her. Perceiving his situation and to avoid his looks, Satarapa moved aside, Brahma however being unable to move, but still desirous of seeing her, caused a face to spring out in the direction in which she sought to avoid his glances, and as she changed her position four times, a corresponding number of faces proceeded from Brahma's head. The goddess Saraswati is the wife of Brahma, on whose tongue she is supposed to reside. She is the goddess of speech, and to her false witnesses perjurers, and liars make their oblations of cakes, rice and milk, to expiate and seek pardon for the venial offence of falsehood.

P. ORR AND SONS,

(ESTABLISHED A. D. 1849.)

MANUFACTURING JEWELLERS AND SILVERSMITHS,

MOUNT ROAD, MADRAS.

THE CELEBRATED ESTABLISHMENT

For the Manufacture of the fashionable Gold and Silver embossed

"SWAMI" JEWELLERY;

TEA, DESSERT, AND BREAKFAST SERVICES;

AND GOLD OR SILVER ADDRESS CASKETS.

The London "COURIER" of January 30th, 1875, says : " We have recently been "afforded the opportunity of inspecting several cases of silver dessert "knives, forks, and spoons manufactured by the well-known firm of "P. ORR and SONS, Madras. The articles for the most part are exceed- "ingly massive, and the workmanship is elaborate and artistic, nearly "every piece of silver varies in design, and is wrought to represent a "heathen deity,—hence the name " Swami" work, by which this class of "goods is known. As remarkable specimens of native manufacture they " merit close examination."

"SWAMI" Jewellery is particularly massive and effective in appearance, and is much sought after and admired both in Europe and America.

The workmanship is peculiar to the artisans of Southern India, and when well made and properly finished, the articles are alike remarkable as specimens of skill and patience displayed by native workmen as for their sterling quality, and the accuracy and precision in which each character is pourtrayed.

i

P. ORR AND SONS

SWAMI JEWELLERY.—(*Continued.*)

The Lockets and other smaller articles each bear a distinct representation of a heathen deity, whilst the larger pieces, such as Bracelets and Necklets combine quite a series of similar representations from the varied subjects comprised in the Hindoo Pantheon.

THE JEWELLERY CONSISTS OF

BRACELETS, NECKLETS, EARRINGS, PENDANTS, BROOCHES, VELVET SLIDES, RINGS, PINS, STUDS, SOLITAIRES AND SLEEVE LINKS.

Complete "Swami" suites for Ladies prepared, and special attention paid to the Selection of the " Swamies" to ensure the greatest variety possible.

Silver " Swami" Jewellery made only to order.

THE "INDIAN" JEWEL CASKET.

Is calculated to form a very complete, handsome, and appropriate Complimentary or Wedding Present. It contains one deep gauntlet "Swami" Bracelet, one ten medallion "Swami" Bracelet, one "Swami" Necklet, one pair "Swami" Earrings, one pair "Swami" Solitaires, one "Swami" Pendant and one "Swami" Velvet Slide, one silver Bouquet holder, one filagree silver Card case, one filagree silver Necklet, one pair filagree silver Bracelets, one pair filagree silver Earrings, one pair filagree silver Hairpins, one filagree silver Brooch, and one filagree silver Comb ornament.

"SWAMI" BRACELETS.

In the manufacture of these articles we confine ourselves exclusively to working in sovereign or 22 carat gold. The Bracelets are exceedingly rich and handsome, and are made of different sizes and shapes. The six medallion flexible pattern is perhaps the most popular; each medallion being exquisitely chased and illustrating some distinct subject of Hindoo Mythology. Special care is paid to the finish of each character with the view of rendering them faithful representations of the particular deities they are intended to personate, that even to those unacquainted with the country and its associations they can scarcely fail to convey a tolerably correct idea of their respective originals.

P. ORR AND SONS
SWAMI JEWELLERY.—*(Continued.)*

"CASTE" BRACELETS.

Contain illustrations of Snake charmers, Barbers, Toddy drawers, and Bearers, Water Curriers, Lapidaries, Horsekeepers, Grass Cutters, Dhobies, (washermen) Road-makers, Scavengers, &c. These Bracelets resemble both in style and appearance the Swami Bracelets, and were originally designed, and are manufactured solely by us, to meet the religious prejudices of those who object to the native "Swamies" as a method of personal ornamentation.

"SWAMI" NECKLETS.

With one, three, or five pendants, also with a treble row of graduated medallions, with pendants, or single row flexible medallions, forming a handsome and effective collarette.

"SWAMI" PENDANTS.

In a variety of shapes and sizes: oval or the fashionable Lozenge shape, Embossed on both sides or with plain gold or glass backs.

"CASTE" PENDANTS.

In similar sizes and shapes to the above, with characters *en suite* with the "Caste" Bracelets.

"SWAMI" EARRINGS.

Various new designs, one, two or three drops, Shield shape, Lozenge shape, and other patterns.

"SWAMI" BROOCHES.

Of different sizes, open or solid work.

"SWAMI" SUITES.

For Gentlemen, comprising Studs, Collar Button, and Solitaires or Sleeve Links.

"SWAMI" SUNDRIES.

Include Scarf pins, Waistcoat buttons, Signet rings, large size Solitaires for ladies, and velvet slides.

P. ORR AND SONS
SILVER "SWAMI" GOODS.

THE
COMPLETE "SWAMI" SERVICE
FOR "AFTERNOON" GARDEN PARTIES,

Comprises twelve each Tea cups and saucers, twelve Tea spoons, Sugar tongs, Teapot, Sugar basin and Cream jug, two large Salvers, each capable of containing six Tea cups and saucers, and one smaller Salver adapted for the Teapot, Sugar basin and cream jug ; the whole worked in high relief with characters illustrating native deities and contained in a beautifully polished cabinet, with silver mountings and folding doors.

We recently had the honor of preparing a similar set to the above in execution of an order from H. H. the Gaekwar of Baroda, and subsequently presented by His Highness, to His Royal Highness the Prince of Wales, and regarding which Sir T. Madava Row writes :

" I avail myself of this opportunity to reiterate my unqualified approval of the " design and execution of the Tea Service, His Highness the Maharajah has presented " it to His Royal Highness the Prince of Wales. His Royal Highness and Staff, and " in fact every body who has seen it, have been struck with its workmanship."

This opinion was also communicated to us personally by various members of His Royal Highness's Staff, with the addition that as a complete and effective piece of work, it was vastly superior, and was accordingly appreciated by His Royal Highness beyond anything else presented to him, during his tour in India.

"SWAMI" TEA SERVICES.

Richly embossed " Swami" Tea Services, consisting of Teapot, Sugar Basin and Cream Jug. The characters on these articles convey a vivid impression of a native religious procession continued from one article to the other, the whole forming a complete train, and combining illustrations of cars, banners, elephants, camels and the other indispensable characteristics of a native gala day.

iv

P. ORR AND SONS
SILVER SWAMI GOODS.—(*Continued.*)

THE "MADRAS" DESSERT CABINET.

Is a beautifully polished case, with plate glass top and front, and silver mountings, and is fitted with 12 each " Swami" Dessert knives and forks, 12 "Swami" Fruit spoons, 12 "Swami" Dessert spoons, 12 " Swami" Tea spoons and 12 each " Swami" Fish eating knives and forks. The whole elaborately chased and finished in best style.

"SWAMI" DESSERT KNIVES & FORKS.

In sets of 6 and 12 each knives and forks in polished cases. In addition to the usual " Swami" each of these articles contain illustrations of quite a mass of cognate native subjects, including Hindoo Pagodas (Temples) processional and other transit cars, jugglers, snake charmers and numerous beasts, birds, and plants, peculiar to the tropics.

"SWAMI" FISH EATING KNIVES AND FORKS.

In similar sets to the above.

"SWAMI" FRUIT SPOONS.

The handles of these Spoons are exquisitely chased, the upper portion of each representing a heathen deity with name engraved, the bowls being richly gilt and engraved with native subjects. In sets of two, four and six in morocco case.

"SWAMI" DESSERT SPOONS.

In similar style and sets to the above.

"SWAMI" TEA SPOONS.

With richly chased cobra or Swamy handles and gilt bowls. In sets of six and twelve in morocco cases.

"SWAMI" SUNDRIES.

Include Muffineers, Napkin rings, Goblets, Tea cups and saucers, Whistles, Ramasawmies, Snuff boxes, Card cases and Children's Presentation Plate.

P. ORR AND SONS

SILVER SWAMI GOODS.—*(Continued.)*

In the event of any of the above goods not being on hand, we shall be happy to make to order or design and submit estimate for the same description of work in any article not enumerated above.

Orders by post receive prompt and careful attention.

ILLUSTRATED CATALOGUES WITH PRICE LIST, POST FREE ON APPLICATION.

VIZAGAPATAM WARE.

A choice assortment of Carved Ivory Buffaloe horn and Sandalwood boxes, Back-gammon boards, Knitting cases, Needle books, Watch cases, Stationery cabinets, Ink-stands, Blotting pads, &c.

P. ORR & SONS,
Madras.

CPSIA information can be obtained at www.ICGtesting.com
Printed in the USA
LVOW11*1916051113

360110LV00025B/1254/P